URAM MONOGRAPHS No. 2

Jesus Christ As Ultimate Reality and Meaning
A Contribution to the Hermeneutics of Conciliar Theology

Tibor Horvath, S.J.

URAM, Regis College: Toronto, Ontario, Canada

Published by the Association of Concern for Ultimate Reality and Meaning conjoint
with the International Society for the Study of Human Ideas on Ultimate Reality
and Meaning, U.R.A.M. is a trade mark for both the Association and the
International Society. Address, URAM, Regis College,
15 St. Mary Street, Toronto, Ontairo, Canada M4Y 2R5.

ISBN 0–9697533–1–4

Tibor Horvath, S.J.

Jesus Christ as Ultimate Reality and Meaning.
A Contribution to the Hermeneutics of Counciliar Theology.

Theology, History, Hermeneutics, URAM, Ultimate Reality and Meaning,

1. Theology

Typeset by University of Toronto Press Incorporated
Printed by University of Toronto Press Incorporated, Toronto, Canada.

Orders: University of Toronto Press Incorporated
5201 Dufferin Street, Downsview, Ontario, Canada M3H 5TS.

As a *leitfaden* for research the following threefold description of ultimate reality and meaning has been adopted by URAM Research:

—ultimate, i.e. that to which one reduces or relates everything and that which one does not relate or reduce to anything else (in the ontological sense);

—that hermeneutical principle which is not interpreted any further, yet in the light of which everything else is interpreted (in the epistemological sense)

—that supreme value for which someone would sacrifice everything and which one would not lose for anything (in the ethical sense)

Contents

Contents

1.
Foreword

The history of this little book began on one day in 1982 when a non-Catholic student of theology came to Regis College, a Roman Catholic Jesuit College, Toronto, and asked for STL, Licentiate in Sacred Theology. STL is a degree which before Vatican II could be granted only to a Roman Catholic theologian who took the oath against Modernism promising that he accepts and will follow all that the infallible magisterium of the Roman Catholic Church is teaching.

Originally an academic licentiate meant the status of someone who, after having completed certain academic requirements, was allowed to teach independently of his master's direct supervision without having the title "Doctor." It was an authorization for teaching at universities and only later when, independently of the Church, more and more theological faculties and universities were established by heads of state did it become a degree granted only by Ecclesiastical faculties and universities erected or approved by the Holy See. The purpose of these ecclesiastical institutions stated in John-Paul II's Encyclical *Sapientia Christiana*, dated on April 15, 1979, is to "cultivate and promote their own discipline and especially deepen knowledge of Christian revelation and of matters connected with it considering the most recent progress of the sciences and to present them to the people of the present day in a manner adapted to various cultures in close communion with the hierarchy on the work of evangelization" (art. 3).

After Vatican II seminaries and theological schools tried to get closer relations with the state universities of their region and students of theological studies were more interested in acquiring "civil degrees" than "ecclesiastic ones." Yet with the decreasing number of seminarians more and more laymen and laywomen enroled in theological studies. And so was in Toronto where TST, the Toronto School of Theology was founded in 1969. TST is made up seven theological schools of Toronto, the Emmanuel College of the United Church of Canada, the Knox College of the Presbyterian Church of Canada, Regis College of the Jesuits of the Upper Canada Province, the Roman Catholic Diocesan St. Augustine's Seminary, the High Anglican Trinity College, the

Roman Catholic Basilian Theology Faculty of the University of St. Michael's College and the Law Anglican Wycliffe College. Keeping one's own tradition each confers its own Master and Doctoral Degrees — in conjunction with the University of Toronto — fully recognized by the founding members.

When in 1982 the Anglican student from the Trinity College asked for STL from Regis College, the only one in Toronto having the granting power, his intention was that by returning to his homeland in Africa, he would establish an interdenominational Christian School of Theology. Having a licentiate from a Roman Catholic Theological Faculty he hoped that the Roman Catholic bishops of his country would have less difficulty allowing their seminarians to study together with other non–Catholic African students of theology. Meanwhile women in increasing number have received an MA (Master of Arts in Theology) and ThM (Master of Theology) from Regis College and other colleges of TST and thus were entitled to apply to Regis College for a Licentiate in Sacred Theology if they wished. After some investigation it turned out that by this time the Jesuit Gregorian University in Rome had already granted the Licentiate to non-catholic students male and female alike without requiring the oath against Modernism.

On the basis of the mutual recognition of the degrees granted by the founding colleges of the TST, some faculty members of Regis College had the opinion that without any further requirement STL should be granted to any students of the Toronto School of Theology who had received MA or ThD of PhD in Theology and who asks for that degree. Since such a procedure would have made STL rather insignificant, after lengthy debate the view prevailed that the comprehensive exam in Theology, an abbreviated form of the earlier Jesuit *examen ad gradum*, required by the students of Regis College, be required from any non-Regis student who asks for an STL, in addition to one course to be taken at Regis College.

The above mentioned Encyclical *Sapientia Christiana* recognizes the Licentiate as "an academic degree which enables one to teach in a major seminary or equivalent school" and that competent ecclesiastical authority may state that the Licentiate is a required degree for filling various ecclesiastical posts (art 50, par 1, 2). It then seemed that a course on Conciliar Theology of the twenty–one Ecumenical Councils would be the most appropriate way of familiarizing a non-Catholic theologian with the history and the doctrinal development of the Roman Catholic theology.

The first course on Conciliar Theology at Regis was offered in 1987–1988. Since until 1990 no English translation of the complete text of the twenty-one Ecumenical Councils was available, most of the students had to rely on secondary sources and inadequate, sometimes biassed translations without being able to be exposed directly to the whole conciliar texts.

This unfortunate situation came to an end in 1990 when under the initiative and direction of the Rev. Norman P. Tanner, S.J., lecturer in Medieval History at Campion Hall, Oxford University and in Church History at Heythrop

College, London University, 29 Jesuit scholars of the British Isles finished the English translation of the complete original conciliar texts published by G. Alberigo and others in 1972.

Decrees of the Ecumenical Councils, published by Sheed & Ward and Georgetown University Press, 1990, was the first attempt ever made to make, after the Bible the most important documents of the Catholic Faith available to the faithful in a living language of our days. The translators, well versed in classical languages and theology, in an exquisite English made it possible that he conciliar texts make a direct impact on English readers and let them sense how the Church, confronting new questions and problems as a community, tries to update itself beginning with the first Council of Nicaea and up to Vatican II.

The result of teaching Conciliar Theology for over six years is presented here as a manual, or *leitfaden* to *Decrees of the Ecumenical Councils*. It is dedicated to my graduate students who took or are going to take the course, to my colleagues interested in introducing a new course in theology, to group leaders discussing the history of the Church and its way of solving problems and finally to directors instructing people of other faith or religions interested in the Catholic Church. It is my hope that by following the Church through its councils in search of finding the right answer to the challenges of an ever changing world, we discover the history of the Church as the history of our life and find inspiration to move history ahead towards resurrection.

2.

Conciliar Theology as a Theological Discipline

The task of the *conciliar* theology is to scrutinize the theology of the Church as a community employed during its twenty-one ecumenical councils. It is not just a history of the political background and the psychological motivation with its sociological conditions which had influenced the outcome of each council. Rather it is a search for the final hermeneutical principle to which all secondary hermeneutical principles are reduced and related and which is not related or reduced to any further principles. It is a search for a problem-solving paradigm in the light of which any new emerging problem is resolved. Its main concern is not only what the councils say, but also why the councils say what they say, and why the members of the councils came to the conclusions they reached.

If one can study the theology of a theologian, for example, St. Augustine, Thomas Aquinas, Martin Luther, Karl Barth, Karl Rahner and so on, one should study more so the theology of an assembly of the leading theologians of an age, working together in conjunction and competition to let the whole council, like a jury, select and vote in favor of one answer as the *ortho-doxa*, 'the right opinion.' The theology of the councils is more the theology of the Church than the theology of any single theologian. The acceptance of a council as an ecumenical council means precisely that the theology employed by that council is not just a local and temporary theology, but an universal theology inserted in the organic unity of the ever-growing theology of the Church, which, as we will see, is the Church's ever-growing understanding of the one and the same Jesus Christ.

As a note we want to mention here that *conciliar* theology should not be confused with conciliar theory prevailing in the 15th century claiming that supreme authority in the Church belongs to the Council above the Pope. It is not even a conciliar theology in the sense of the English word of conciliatory, soothing, or placating opposing views and moods. It is not even just a theology of the councils. Rather it is a search for the theological method used by the councils in answering questions proposed by the time. It is a form of new theological discipline not yet forming part of the theological curriculum. To

5

underline the distinctiveness of this new curriculum we would like to use consistently the word counciliar theology instead of conciliar theology.

The counciliar theology should be made up of three courses
- Counciliar Theology I: General Survey of the Church's 21 Ecumenical Councils;
- Counciliar Theology II: Textual analysis of the Church's Ecumenical Councils;
- Counciliar Theology III: Hermeneutical Analysis of the Church's Ecumenical Councils.

A more detailed description of the three courses could be as follows:
Counciliar Theology I: Geographic setting, historical circumstances and theological issues prompting the convocation. Teaching: central and accessory topics. Doctrinal dynamics moving from the first council to the twenty first with key words for each one. Church History reflected in the Ecumenical Councils as History of Faith in Jesus Christ.

Counciliar Theology II: Five councils studied in depth: two, for example, from the first millennium, two from the second millennium, plus Vatican II; History of the formation of the text; influential theologians, parties and schools involved in the debates; participants' way of arguing, method of accepting emendations, final redaction of the counciliar text; impact of one council on the following ones (*Wirkungsgeschichte*).

Counciliar Theology III: Search for different problem-solving paradigms, operative in the councils, like *analogia fidei* (analogy of faith), *analogia entis* (analogy of being), *non solum ... sed etiam* (not only ... but also), Christ as primary analogate, removal (the substance of the bread, for example) and replacement (e. g., the body of Christ) as a way of unifying divine with human; Scriptural passages and references used by the councils and their applications; Search for secondary hermeneutical principles implicitly used by the councils; Difference between secular humanistic (non-theistic and non-Christological), theistic (non-Christological), and Christological interpretation of the counciliar documents; Hermeneutics of the Word of God (inspiration: accepting the human words as the Word of God, cf. 1 Thess 2, 13), hermeneutics of the Magisterium of the Church (dogmatic definitions, infallible and fallible teachings of the Church); Hermeneutics employed by human societies, for example, in the Constitution and the Amendments to the Constitution of U.S.A, or decision-making process in international corporations, etc., and the appropriate hermeneutics of the councils.

For its pioneering nature the present essay is limited in scope. After some consideration of hermeneutics in general we present a short history of different hermeneutical solutions before the Council of Nicaea I (325) applied to the problem of how to combine faith in Jesus Christ with faith in one God. And then we will intimate the Church's growing understanding of Christ through the ecumenical councils beginning with Nicaea which had established the final principle of any Christian hermeneutics, sc., Jesus Christ, the real God and real man as the ultimate reality and meaning, and concluding with Vatican II.

3.
What is Hermeneutics and How Does It Work?

Hermeneutics is a discipline of interpretation. It suggests a certain set of rules of interpretation organized hierarchically and interpreted by one last principle which is interpreting the rest but is not interpreted by any other, at least for a given time. It is that final principle in the light of which one understands whatever one understands. This is the epistemological function of the idea of the ultimate reality and meaning which we accept and posit for ourselves. The ultimacy of this idea is obviously conditioned by tradition, education, by the world we encounter, the experiences we have had and by the problems our mind is registering in its search for knowing more and more.

The use of such a principle is universal though not always reflectively recognized and linguistically formulated. It is one of the most basic activities of the human mind which always tries to relate the unknown to the already known. Lack of understanding is nothing else but a current inability of finding relation between what we know and what we would like to know.

Obviously, that we know and what we know is not always at our disposal. What was unknown yesterday may become known today. Moreover, often we find problems which we just cannot solve any more in the light of our known 'old' axioms or concepts of ultimate reality and meaning. Experiences which were interpreted in the light of our old concept of ultimate reality and meaning now are challenging the validity of the same concept of ultimate reality and meaning. Suddenly the interpreted turns out to be the interpreter and the interpreter the interpreted. Such a conflict between our experience and the old ultimate hermeneutical principle is not as rare as one would like to admit. It is the outcome of the dynamics of the human mind trying to grasp the whole and break through the constructed networks of a system which until recently was able to domesticate any new phenomenon. The ultimate principle of our hermeneutics is not a static permanent light which lasts for ever and can penetrate any darkness we may encounter. It is rather like the way we are, personal, fragile, constantly tested by new experiences, particularly through other peoples' evidences, beliefs and concepts of ultimate reality and meaning.

The creation and formation of the concept of ultimate reality and meaning is one of the most original and personal activities of each human brain. No one else can understand for us. We have to understand for ourselves. What a machine can do the human brain cannot: take in words without understanding. Understanding must be carried out by ourselves for ourselves and that over and over again.

Consequently, understandings are as many as human beings are. We can say that the idea of ultimate reality and meaning with its basic function of acting as a supreme judge of interpretation is as varied as the number of human persons who ever existed on earth. Nevertheless, we could reduce this indefinite number of ideas of ultimate reality and meaning to three fundamental models: space, time and person. The first uses infinite space, the second endless time and the third an infinite person as ultimate reality and meaning.

It seems that society does not really function as an independent model in addition to the models of space, time and person in our concepts of ultimate reality and meaning. The reason is that society is either viewed as a spatial extension of many units, in which one person is acting like the smallest unit in an endless space, or the society itself is elevated to a superhuman personality conceived no otherwise than as a person in singular form (Horvath, 1977b, pp. 324–325).

Spatial interpretation visualizes the ultimate reality and meaning as infinite space, and the key words used are context, milieu, horizon, perspective, etc. It is based on our ability of sight, in virtue of it we want to see everything in space-extension. We want to extend particular perception into a total perception in order to improve our seeing either by microscope or telescope installed here on earth or placed on spaceships, and so on. The progress in understanding according to this model is a progress in expanding horizons over horizons.

The time model is based on our temporal existence. To understand something is to know its beginning and its end. When we ask for information we ask for date of birth, names of parents, profession, etc. We want to know where does something or someone come from, where does one go, and what does one try to achieve in the future. It is a knowledge 'from where' (efficient cause) and 'to where' (final cause). The space and time models of ultimate reality and meaning are the scientific ideas of ultimate reality and meaning. It is an understanding of locations and influences by efficient and final causes.

The person model of ultimate reality and meaning is based on our existence as a person, who is considered to be irreducible to anything else. He/she is the explanation of him/herself. Since one is a person, he/she does what she/he wants. Therefore he/she is free: free of his/her location, of his/her efficient and final causes. It is not a scientific but a personal knowledge. It is different from explanations offered by psychology or sociology, which, as science, look for general, relatively universal categories by way of explanation. The person model interpretation of ultimate reality and meaning distinguishes the hermeneutics of faith from hermeneutics of science.

We should notice that the person model interpretation of ultimate reality and meaning is not just the acceptance of a person as a horizon of understanding, as can happen in a certain degree of love. Rather it is positing a person as the universal meaning of everything which is to be understood and/or can ever be understood. A person appears within the horizons of persons as the final hermeneutical principle in the light of which not only each person but the whole universe is to be understood.

The three models, space, time and person, interact on the various levels of science, art and faith. The distinction emerges when one model takes up the role of the final one and becomes the axiom in the light of which the other two are explained. In one instance space can be the meaning of a person, and in another the person the meaning of space. For the first, space is God. For the second, God has created space. And the same is true about time.

Positing a person as ultimate reality and meaning means that both the person and the ultimate reality and meaning mutually assume the characteristics of each other. Since the notion of reality and meaning is not the same for each one of us so the notion of person too presents an unlimited variety. Yet there is a common parameter in each. Each can address ultimate reality and meaning as 'thou,' which distinguishes faith from science, the believer from the non-believer, the believer as worshipping from the believer as measuring.

As in any activity of understanding so in any positing an idea of ultimate reality and meaning we have to distinguish the mental process, the 'activity by which' one is positing ultimate reality and meaning, from that which is posited as ultimate reality and meaning. The first is dependent on the human brain and the second, the 'what' one conceives as ultimate reality and meaning, is posited as independent of one's own brain. The two, the 'by what,' e. gr. faith, and the 'what,' e. gr. God, cannot be completely separated, since human person as person and God as person can be encountered and recognized by other(s) as other only through the activity of affirming the other as other. This is why God cannot be encountered as person except in faith. Revelation and faith are, therefore, inseparable. But so in any personal knowledge is the person who knows and the person who is known. Our knowledge is an intersubjective – affirming other subjects as others – knowledge in the world.

By analyzing the nature of the act of positing a person as the ultimate reality and meaning or affirming God as a person, we find that such an activity does not have the structure of deduction or induction, but rather the combination of both. It is theoretical and practical, speculative and experimental, and follows the pattern of discovery (Horvath, 1980, pp. 144–163). It is different from reflective, systematic investigation, since it does not conclude in the form of a syllogism. It is a trying and testing process of finding out which one of the various conceivable concepts of ultimate reality and meaning has a greater interpreting and problem solving power in competition with other interpreting but non-interpreted principles for the anomalies perceived in the surrounding world. It is a search and affirmation of what reality in the final analysis is for one individual.

An unambiguous interpretation of the idea of ultimate reality and meaning based on a person model is found in the books of the Bible. The God of the Bible is the ultimate reality and meaning to whom everything is related and who is not related or reduced to anything or to anyone else. He is that hermeneutical principle in the light of which the Bible writers tried to understand and interpret everything and to fight rigorously against any attempt of doing otherwise, labelled as idolatry. For them Yahweh was the supreme value for whom one should sacrifice everything, even one's own son or life, since no true believer would not want to lose him for anything else. Yahweh was not a human being. He was invisible. He was not of this world, nevertheless, he loved his elected people. Yet he was not one of them, because he was far above anyone and everything.

This concept of ultimate reality and meaning, this faith, had been challenged when Jesus of Nazareth was believed to belong to God in a way such as no one ever was before and no one ever would be after him. He had been seen as a new hermeneutical principle in the light of which not only humans but God too had to be understood by us. There was a new concept of ultimate reality and meaning that involved not only God but also Jesus' human existence.

The transition from the old concept of ultimate reality and the meaning to the new one, the unambiguous acceptance of Jesus Christ as the final principle of hermeneutics (cf. recognition of the divinity of Christ) took more than a day or a year. Even when it was done, the challenge (opposition from outside and 'temptation' from inside) never passed away. During its two thousand years of history the Church had to test again and again the problem-solving power of its new hermeneutical principle. The primordial 'anomaly' prompting the Christian shift of paradigm was the mystery of Christ which solves anomalies by intensifying them. For being an 'anomaly' for all solutions it remains the unsurpassable problem-solving power throughout history.

4.

The New Testament Challenge to the Old Concept of Ultimate Reality and Meaning

It was during the first century of our era that the concept of ultimate reality and meaning of the Old Testament was challenged. The new concept was still based on a person model yet the faith in Yahweh was gradually shifted to a human being, a Jew from Nazareth, called Jesus. The writers of the books of the New Testament had transferred to him more and more of those functions, attributes which prior to him were reserved only to the God of Israel.

Mark, for example, attributes to Jesus of Nazareth the title of Son of God (Mk 1, 1), the title of the Lord of the Sabbath (Mk 2, 28), the power of forgiving sins (Mk 2, 1–2), of calming the sea and winds (Mk 4, 41) which previously obeyed only God (Gen 1, 2; Ps 89, 10; Job 9,8; 26, 12-13; Is 63, 12–13), of sending angels (Mk 13, 27), all exclusive powers of Yahweh.

Matthew too places Jesus above the level of creatures on a level equal to God by reason of his power of knowing and by reason of what he knows (Mt 11, 27). His sonship is so mysterious that Peter could know only by a special divine revelation (Mt 16, 16) which in the author's understanding deserved the high priest's condemnation as blasphemy (Mt 26, 63–66) for claiming a divine prerogative implying the scorning and abasing of God (Horvath, 1975, p. 190).

Luke calls Jesus Lord, i.e., Kurios, the Greek name of Yahweh in the Septuagint (Lk 7, 13; 10, 1. 17. 39. 41; 11. 1. 39).

The fourth gospel presents him as pre-existent to creation, identical with the Logos, the Word who was God (Jn 1, 1). Jesus was one with the Father (Jn 10, 30) and equal with God the Father in acting (Jn 5, 17; 8, 18; 14, 10) in knowing (10, 15) and in being (5, 18; 10, 30. 33. 36; 14, 7. 10. 20; 17, 21). And the listeners seemed to understand what he was talking about, since according to the author they wanted to stone him because he made himself equal to God (Jn 10,33; 5, 18).

Prior to the writings of the gospels Paul, the apostle, and his communities, confessed Jesus of Nazareth's preexistence in the form of God (Phil 2, 6–11); 1 Tim 3, 16), his action in creation (1 Cor 8,6). They prayed to him as to their Lord (2 Cor 12, 8; 1 Th 3, 12; 2, Th 3, 2) since in him the fullness of God's nature was present (Col 2, 9).

11

The origin of Christianity, indeed, can be placed in the discovery of a new concept of ultimate reality and meaning based on some unique experience which challenged the old one and created a conflict between two concepts of ultimate reality and meaning, sc., God, the Father of Israel, and Jesus of Nazareth, as real man and real God.

For an outside observer the conflict looked like a dispute over Jewish superstition (Acts 25, 19) and the dispute should be logically solved in favor of the Jewish official labelling Jesus as sorcerer, who 'enticed Israel to Apostasy' (Babylonian Talmud, Sanhedrin, 43a; Strack, Billerbeck, 1922, 1, 36–43). And, indeed, it seems that only since M. de Jonde's book entitled *Jeschuah der klassische Jüdischer Mann, Zerstörung des kirchlichen, Enthüllung des jüdischen Jesusbildes*, Berlin 1904, could Jesus be considered by Jewish authors as a classical Jew, a national hero, without having a new concept of ultimate reality and meaning different from that of his contemporary fellow countrymen. The new concept of ultimate reality and meaning was a 'discovery' of his followers.

But the question remains. If Jesus of Nazareth is not considered as the discoverer and revealer of a new concept of ultimate reality and meaning and consequently the founder of Christianity, who was the one who discovered and made the new idea of ultimate reality and meaning acceptable to many. Certainly it was neither Mark, nor Matthew, John, or Paul, since the form criticism of the Gospel writings suggests that the new concept existed before them. But then who proposed the new concept of ultimate reality and meaning remains the lasting problem for New Testament scholars.

One could ask whether anyone would be accepted as a charismatic religious leader without having a new concept of ultimate reality and meaning. What else would make one a genius in religion if not precisely having discovered a new concept of God which is grasped and apprehended as such by his/her followers?

It is beyond any doubt that the concept of ultimate reality and meaning presented in the books of the New Testament is revolutionarily new. It is, indeed, astonishing and baffling. God is not to be found anymore 'outside' of Jesus of Nazareth. Anyone who has seen him has seen the Father (Jn 14, 9–10; 12, 45). He is the image, the likeness (eikon) of the invisible God in whom all the fullness of God dwells (Col 1, 15. 19; 2, 9; 2 Cor 4, 4–6). There is nowhere else to go to find God besides Christ who cannot be reduced to someone or something outside of him (cf Jn 6, 68–69). For him one is ready to sacrifice everything and would not want to lose him for anything (Phil 3, 7–8).

One can expect that of all those who did not reject offhand the revolutionary newness of such an idea of ultimate reality and meaning there were some who tried to explain it in the light of the old concept of ultimate reality and meaning. They denied the ultimacy of the new one by reducing it to the old one professing only Yahweh. Yet there were others who confessed Jesus Christ within a 'Trinitarian' God as the new hermeneutical principle solving any problem between God and the world. They called the ones who 'preferred' the old concept of ultimate reality and meaning heretics ('the choosers' *aireomai*), and named themselves 'orthodox,' the ones determined to move 'straight' ahead. Yet the Arian 'temptation' of looking for God 'outside' of Jesus of Nazareth is too human and cannot simply be left behind once for all. It will never cease to challenge the 'orthodoxy' of the new faith.

5.

The History of Hermeneutical Solutions Combining Faith in Jesus Christ with the Faith in One God in the Light of the Old Concepts of Ultimate Reality and Meaning Before 325

The question whether Jesus of Nazareth can be considered as ultimate reality and meaning was negatively answered by all those who tried to resolve the Jesus-problem either by referring him to Old Testament (Jewish hermeneutics), or Pagan religious (Gnostic hermeneutics) and Platonic philosophical (Platonic hermeneutics) categories. For these Jesus Christ was not the ultimate reality and meaning, i.e., that to which the faithful reduce and relate everything and that which the faithful would not reduce and relate to anything else outside of him. He was not the last hermeneutical principle in the light of which believers should understand whatever they understand. Rather Jesus himself was to be reduced and related to something or someone else, sc., the God of Old Testament (Jewish Christians) or to the God in general (Gentile Christians). The Church historian would distinguish among them the monarchianists and trinitarianists.

5.1 Monarchianists
The monarchianists kept the one God as the ultimate reality and meaning who was either transcendent to Jesus or personally identical with him. The first were the transcendental and the second the immanent monarchianists.

5.1.2 Transcendental Monarchianists
The transcendental monarchianists had Jewish as well Gentile Christian followers.

5.1.2.1
Jewish Christian transcendental monarchianists were among others the Ebionites, the 'poor men' who lived on the east side of the Jordan. They looked upon Jesus only as an angel, like the Seraphim of Isaiah (*The Ascension of Isaiah*, 6, 3) or Angel Michael (Hermes, *Similitudes*, 8, 2, 3). A Christology of the Judaic Christians can be detected in the writings of Paul of Samosata too. For him Christ was a man like other man, different from the prophets only in degree.

Yet when the Spirit had descended upon him, he became God's adopted son (Adoptionism).

5.1.2.2
Obviously the Gentile Christian transcendental monarchianists sought for Christological problem-solving categories in their own philosophical tradition. Accordingly they related Jesus either to gnostic categories giving to Jesus a preeminent role in leading the spiritual back to God (Story, 1981, pp. 279–296) or to the Platonic idea of God. Thus Jesus was recognized as an emissary of the Father, who appeared like a shadow (docetism) of the real Platonic ultimate One. This was the Christology of Marcion's followers, the Marcionites.

5.1.2.3
Arius is the most prominent monarchianist Gentile Christian. He placed great emphasis on the unity of God. God the Father is the only ultimate and Jesus as man is subordinated to him (subordinationism). Being Jesus a creature he could not be ultimate reality and meaning. Otherwise God would be composite.

5.1.3 Immanent Monarchianists
To avoid any composition in God the immanent monarchianists had simply reduced Jesus Christ the Son to the Father by making him completely identical with the Father. So for Sabellius, Praxeas, Noetus, Patripassionists, and in general for the Sabellianists or Modalists, Jesus could not be ultimate reality and meaning. He was just a different mode of the one and the same God.

5.2 *Pre-Nicaean Trinitarianists*

5.2.1 Tertullian
Trinitarianists named the Father, the Son and the Holy Spirit as each belonging to the category of the divinity, lordship and sanctifying power of the Godhead. God was the Son but 'temporally.' The full Godhead inhabited him. For Tertullian not the Son but the Father was the ultimate reality and meaning, since the Trinity for him was only the result of a unity unfolding into Trinity. Just as the root brings forth stem, the sun its beam, so the Father too the Son. Therefore, to understand the Father we do not need the Son. For Tertullian to see the Son was not the same as seeing the Father (cf Jn 14, 9). And Origen believed something similar.

5.2.2 Origen
Due to his strong Platonic tendencies, unlike Tertullian, Origen could exclude all materiality from the Son, yet the Son seemed to remain inferior. The Father is God (*auto-theos, 'o theos*), whereas the Son is god by participation (*metochè*).

The Father surpasses the Son like the idea of goodness surpasses the good in the sense of the Platonic theory of participation. For Origen the Father is God, the Son is God, yet the Father is divinity itself. The Son is not the divinity itself. If on account of the unfolding for Tertullian the Son was God 'temporally,' for Origen he was God but only by participation. In neither case was Jesus Christ the ultimate reality and meaning.

6.

Christological Interpretation of the 21 Ecumenical Councils

By using old concepts of ultimate reality and meaning the pre-Nicaean hermeneutical solutions failed to combine the Church's faith in Jesus Christ with its faith in one God. They failed to justify the worship of Jesus Christ practised already in the early Christian communities which was a spontaneous manifestation of the great love the faithful felt for Jesus Christ. Indeed, the creative power which formed the apostolic communities was not some sort of spiritual insight but a unique love of Jesus prompting a shift in their idea of ultimate reality and meaning. Such a falling in love with Jesus, the man from Nazareth, considered as God's free gift, is an unusual phenomenon in the history of religions. The author of the letter to the Philippians expressed the common feeling of Jesus' followers by saying that there is nothing that can outweigh the love of Christ and he would suffer the loss of all things and count them all as rubbish just to gain Christ not on the basis of one's righteousness but as a free gift through faith (Eph 3, 8–10). To safeguard and to combine such a worshipping love of Jesus Christ with the great commandment of the monotheistic ultimate reality and meaning 'love your God with all your heart' (Mt 22, 37) was the task of the council of Nicaea. How can a man be worshipped if one believes in one God? This was the problem Nicaea had to face.

6.1

The Council of Nicaea 325: Jesus Christ as Real Man and Real God is the Ultimate Reality and Meaning for the Catholic and Apostolic Church

Arius shared his predecessors' love for Jesus of Nazareth. He placed him on his scale of values as high as he could without challenging the uniqueness of God. He believed that Jesus was born before all ages though not before time. As the first born of any creature he was born out of nothing but not of God. For Arius Jesus was not God. God the Father alone remained ultimate reality and meaning, the last hermeneutical principle in the light of which he interpreted Jesus of Nazareth. Jesus was not the revelation of God. Rather God was the revelation of Jesus Christ. The council of Nicaea found that such a love is not enough to ground the apostolic Church's worship of Jesus Christ and, therefore, reversed Arius' position.

Being the first of its kind Nicaea should serve as a model of learning how to be creative and original in doing theology and solving problems of a changing world in the light of Jesus Christ and of his love. Its concern was not a purely philosophical question. The council's participants did not rely on the 'here and now' of their times. They reflected on their liturgical celebration commemorating both Christ's love for them and their love for him. So they took the baptismal creed of Caesarea which Eusebius of Caesarea had at hand and began to work on it. By omitting and adding words they amended to justify their worship of Christ and to safeguard at the same time their monotheistic faith.

It was found necessary to omit the expressions 'first born of all creatures' and 'before all ages' for having Arian flavor. To correct Arius' words 'born from nothing,' the words 'born of the Father,' and 'from the substance of the father' (cf. Tertullian, *Against Praxeas*, 4, PL 2, 159, and Athanasius, *Orations against Arians*, 1, PG 26, 44) were added. The Lord Jesus Christ, therefore, existed as really as the Father did.

Since for Nicaea the reality of Jesus as a real man was not an issue as later for the council of Chalcedon, this time it was not necessary to mention 'real man of real man.' Their point was that this man is not just a man but God as well. To the Caesarean Creed, therefore, the Nicaean added as its own insertion that Jesus 'is true God of true God,' i.e., really God of a God who is really God. The Greek word *alethinos*, namely, means both true in the ethical sense and real or actual in the ontological sense.

Finally, to express the same in Arian terms, a third statement, parallel to the previous two, sc., 'of the substance of the Father' and 'real God of real God,' the non-biblical term, *homoousios* (of the same essence) was added. The term earlier was used already by Adamantius, an anti-Gnostic writer in his Dialogue *De recta in Deum fide* (The right faith in God) (PG 11, 1717). The introduction of such a term seems necessary if one wants to express his/her view unmistakably in a language the world recognizes as its own. By using the term *homoousios* the council of Nicaea was able to express its biblical faith in the language of its time as clearly as it was possible then. By doing this it opened the way for the successive councils to try to express the meaning of the Christ event in the language of their times.

Quite a few authors studying the Council of Nicaea misunderstood the usefulness of the word *homoousios* (of the same essence). They could not see that precisely by the word *homoousios* the council was able to distance itself from positions like that of the anomoeans (*anomoios* 'no similarity'), or of the homoeans (*homoios* 'similar') and of the homoiousians (homoiousios 'similar essence') who failed to accept Jesus Christ as the ultimate reality and meaning.

Since for the council Jesus Christ was the ultimate reality and meaning, it was not the concept or word *ousia* that gave meaning to Christ but rather Christ to the word. It follows, therefore, that not the classical dictionaries but the context of the Nicaean creed determines the meaning of the word *homoousios*. Its meaning is not different from that of two other expressions, sc., 'of the substance of the Father' and 'true God of true God' i.e., Jesus Christ is God in the same sense as the Father is, and no more or less, since 'there never was a time when he was not' (Tanner, 1990, I, p. 5). Briefly, whatever a Christian thinks or says of God, he or she should think and say of Jesus Christ as well. For Nicaea to understand God was to understand Jesus Christ and not vice versa because Jesus is the revelation of God and in him the Godhead fully dwells. In its creed it used not one but three formulas to affirm Jesus Christ as the ultimate reality and meaning.

By doing this the first ecumenical council reaffirmed the radical novelty of the New Testament books. By declaring that this real man is really God, the man Jesus Christ presented in the Gospels has been laid as 'corner stone,' the ultimate reality and meaning expressing the 'divinity' of Christ not only in the ontological, but epistemological and ethical-religious sense of the word.

Faith in Jesus Christ was a revolutionary turning point in the history of the ideas of ultimate reality and meaning. By professing this the council of Nicaea did not deny the validity of other concepts or realities. It just affirmed that any concept or reality finds its fulfillment in a person, i.e., Jesus Christ. Jesus Christ the person is the ultimate reality and meaning of everything, concepts and realities included. He is the primary analogate for any theological research and the final problem-solving paradigm for any question. And by the same token, research of any subject matter is Christological research. For the believing Church from now on solving problems of any kind is solving a Christological problem contributing to a further understanding of Christ. Since not just God but Jesus Christ the real man and the real God is the ultimate reality and meaning and problem-solving paradigm, there is no question of God, or of the secular world which is not a question about Christ. And the successive ecumenical councils serve as confirmation of this.

The impact of the affirmation of Jesus Christ as the ultimate reality and meaning will be, indeed, sensed in the future as the Church is facing various attempts challenging the unity and ultimacy of Jesus Christ. The following twenty ecumenical councils are not just simple applications but a further deepening and unearthing of what it means to say that not God but Jesus Christ the real man and real God is the ultimate reality and meaning. In 325 a problem-solving paradigm was laid down once for all and the history of the Church is the ongoing organic unfolding of that simple discovery which is, indeed, the central issue of the New Testament books as well.

6.2

The Church's Growing Understanding of Christ's Mystery Through the Ecumenical Councils: Jesus Christ as Ultimate Reality and Meaning is Further Unfolded

The traditional historical analysis of the various councils is conditioned and motivated by the specific concern of the various theological treatises or the personal interest of a theologian. As a result, the councils are seen in isolation and the doctrinal dynamics moving from the first council to the last one are overlooked. A conciliar theology, interested in seeing what was the main question a council faced and how it could find an answer to it, is able to detect the dynamic unity progressively unfolding the mystery of the ultimacy of Jesus Christ first in regard to Christ himself (understanding the mystery of incarnation, the first eight councils), and later in regard to the world (understanding the mystery of redemption, the last thirteen councils).

We will briefly present the remaining twenty ecumenical councils and indicate how one after the other and all together unfold Christ's role in the world as ultimate reality and meaning. We want to underline that not just the succession but the acceptance of the councils is also relevant. The fact that there are twenty-one accepted by the Roman Catholic Church suggests that those twenty-one councils are expressing its faith in Jesus Christ as the ultimate reality and meaning as well as that they are correct translations of the same faith for the changing world in which the Church lived and which Jesus Christ is progressively redeeming. At the same time they express the expanding life the Church is experiencing under the leadership of the risen Christ.

6.2.1

Constantinople I 381: Holy Spirit Giver of Life: One Cannot Accept Jesus as Ultimate Reality and Meaning Except by the Holy Spirit: Faith in Jesus is Saving

The recognition of Jesus Christ as the ultimate reality and meaning is not a simple creation of one more idea of ultimate reality and meaning. It is against any logic of God is God and not man, and man is man and not God. The numerous pro-Arian councils following the council of Nicaea indicate how difficult it is to combine one's monotheistic faith with the worship of Jesus Christ. The profession that Jesus Christ is God is not just a knowledge, but a grace, a saving event which is possible only by virtue of the holy Spirit, the giver of life. No one can say that 'Jesus is Lord' except by the holy Spirit (1 Cor 12, 3). This faith of the '150 Fathers' was endorsed and expounded by the confession of the divinity of the holy Spirit.

The holy Spirit does not challenge the ultimacy of Jesus Christ but rather enforces it. According to the New Testament the function of the holy Spirit is always pointing to Jesus. Nicaea confessed that the Father is inseparable from Jesus and Constantinople I acknowledged that the Spirit is inseparable from the Father and is worshipped with the Father and the Son together.

As in the Old Testament so in the New Testament also the term 'Spirit,' the *pneuma*, means many disparate realities. It means wind, breath, principle of biological life, moral courage, the new life in Christ, the invisible world, the angels, the devils and God as well. The faith of the Church in the Holy Spirit as a divine person who is to be worshipped relies mostly on John's Gospel calling the Spirit *the* advocate, with a masculine article *'o* opposed to the neutral form of the Greek *to pneuma*, and on the baptismal formula of Mt 28, 19 'baptizing in the name of the Father and of the Son and of the holy Spirit.' Nicaea gave a solid foundation for the worship of the Son but left untouched the question of the holy Spirit. This task was taken up by the First Council of Constantinople.

What is remarkable in Constantinople I is that the participants could profess a faith in the divinity of the holy Spirit against the Pneumatomachi, who denied the divinity of the holy Spirit, without using the terms 'God' or *homoousios*. By doing this the council gave a further glimpse into the mystery of the new ultimacy.

The holy Spirit is *to kurion*, (with a neutral article). In other words, the Spirit is from the category of lordships and belongs to *'o kurios*, to Jesus Christ. Furthermore, since he proceeds from the Father he is to be worshipped and glorified as Jesus Christ and the Father are both worshipped and glorified together. And finally the Spirit is giver of life, the life of faith, the life eternal (Tanner, 1990, I, p. 24). The Spirit is, therefore, not of the category of the creation, but of that of the divinity. He is not created but proceeds from God the Father. Therefore, he is not a servant of God, but a Lord. Furthermore, he is not sanctified but as giver of life he is a sanctifier. Thus the holy Spirit has a divine name, a divine function, a divine origin and is equal to the Father and to the Son. This is remarkable theology professing the holy Spirit as God without using the term 'God,' yet giving solid foundation for worshipping the holy Spirit in the context of the Church's monotheistic faith.

6.2.2

Ephesus 431: Jesus Christ as Real Man and Real God is One; Therefore, There is a Communication of Properties in Jesus, thus Mary is the Mother of God

The council of Ephesus introduces a new way of proceeding in the history of the councils. Instead of taking a creed, it studies various letters written by two fellow bishops and accepts one of them, sc., the second letter of Cyril to Nestorius as being in agreement with Nicaea expressing faith in Jesus Christ as ultimate reality and meaning.

The concept of an infinite God obviously excludes the idea of a mother of God. But instead of subordinating Jesus Christ to the obvious meanings of words and terms, the council of Ephesus rather subjected concepts and terms to the reality of Jesus as God-man, and thus professed again Jesus Christ as the only true ultimate reality and meaning as well as the only final hermeneutical principle. It is in this light that the council re-interpreted ordinary language by giving new meaning to it.

If Mary were not to be called the mother of God, Jesus as man and God would not be one and his ultimacy as real God and real man would be denied. In Christ only his divinity would be ultimate and not his humanity. But precisely because the real man and the real God together is the ultimate, there must be a *communicatio idiomatum*, a communication of properties in Jesus and Mary, the mother of Jesus, had to be called the mother of God (Tanner, 1990, I, p. 58–59). Divine and human properties had to receive denominations from each other. This is a logical outcome of the inseparability of God and man in Jesus Christ.

Jesus Christ as ultimate reality and meaning is an appropriate paradigm to understand and follow the reasoning of the councils. The logics of Ephesus is operative in the council of Chalcedon.

6.2.3

Chalcedon 451: Jesus Christ is Real God and Real Man (Consubstantial with the Father and With Us) without Change and Confusion (against Monophysites) and without Division and Separation (against Nestorians)

As a working document Chalcedon took the doctrinal formula of union between Cyril of Alexandria (stressing unity) and John of Antioch (favoring dualism) dated from April 23, 433. The formula clearly stated that Christ is not only consubstantial with the Father but also consubstantial with us in regard to his humanity. The same one is truly God and truly man (Tanner, 1990, I, p. 86). But by omitting and adding some words Chalcedon further amended it to balance Monophysitism against Nestorianism and Nestorianism against Monophysitism, since both challenged the faith in Jesus Christ, real God and real man as ultimate reality and meaning.

By stressing unity the Monophysites conceived Jesus Christ as a theanthropic being neither God nor man but someone between the two, a mixture of both. Thus God without Jesus Christ was the only ultimate. And the Nestorians on their part keeping divine and human separate divided the two so much that Jesus only as God was the real ultimate. For neither was Jesus the true man the revelation of God.

To make the case of Nicaea stronger Chalcedon inserted from Leo's letter to Flavian, bishop of Constantinople, the words acknowledging Christ, Son and Lord 'only-begotten, in two natures which undergo no confusion, no change' against Monophysites and 'no division, no separation' against Nestorians, 'but rather the property of both natures is preserved' against Monophysites, 'and come together into a single person and a single subsistant being' against Nestorians (Tanner, 1990, I, p. 86). And as if all that were not enough, between Leo's two phrases it had been inserted from Cyril's Second Letter to Nestorius that 'at no point was the difference between the natures taken away through the union,' i.e., neither during his life on earth nor after his resurrection in heaven. Jesus Christ, therefore, as true God and true man remains ultimate reality and meaning for ever.

In terms of theological precision Chalcedon supersedes Nicaea. Chalcedon is, indeed, more than Nicaea. It inductively 'ascends' from less to a more adequate conceptualization. But no council can supersede the faith of Nicaea in positing Jesus Christ as ultimate reality and meaning. Nicaea is more than Chalcedon and other councils which deductively 'descend' from Nicaea as from more to less by explicating only the implications of Nicaea. This is so, since Chalcedon does not witness to a new ultimate reality and meaning but only defends the one posited in Nicaea and explains its meaning for new questions.

The preeminent moment in the history of the councils is not Chalcedon, but Nicaea. The foundation was laid by Nicaea and no council ever can replace Jesus Christ as ultimate reality and meaning without ceasing to be Christian. Any reversal of the Nicaean Creed would mean the end of Christian faith, and could not be labelled 'orthodox,' i.e., those moving ahead but rather 'un-ortho-dox,' i.e., going back to pre-Nicaea, to the pre-New Testament concepts of ultimate reality and meaning. The infallibility of each successive council depends on the infallibility of Nicaea. The unity of the councils, therefore, is based on Nicaea. On account of this relation all councils form an organic unity, a 'collegiality,' mutually and progressively completing each other. Their unity stems continually from one council. The the ecumenical union of Christian denominations is founded on Nicaea. All other councils are its interpretations.

What Chalcedon did was that it sublated the Aristotelian logic of 'yes' or 'no' by the logic of analogy. It overruled the logical incompatibility of 'God is God and not man,' or 'human is human and not God,' and explicitly stated that Jesus is God but at the same time he is not God, because he is a man. Yet at the same time he is not man, but God. And from now on one of the basic problem-solving paradigms of the subsequent councils will be the *not only* (man) *but* (God as well) and the 'either – or' has been replaced by *and* and *and*. Such a hermeneutics is the logical expression of the internal dynamics of the universal catholicity of Christian faith.

It follows, therefore, that no human worldview or system can be alien to a Christology except in its exclusion of others. There is no human language and culture in which Christology is not to be expressed. Otherwise the validity of Jesus Christ the real man and real God as the ultimate reality and meaning is challenged. Jesus Christ is the ultimate reality and meaning of both heaven and earth. It is precisely because Jesus Christ as real God and real man is the ultimate reality and meaning of both the divine and the human that every conceivable system in its positive aspect is not only open to God, but Christ the true God and true man is both its foundation and its meaning.

Chalcedon's hermeneutics is further expounded by Constantinople II.

6.2.4

Constantinople II 553: In Jesus Christ There Is One Subject; the Union of the Two Natures is a Union by Synthesis or by Person, and, Therefore, There is Only One Person, Namely the Lord Jesus Christ, One Member of the Holy Trinity

The second council of Constantinople with its Three Chapters is not just a repetition of Chalcedon and of Ephesus. Rather it is their precision by negation. The 'hypostatic' union of God with man can be more easily approximated by negation, i.e., telling what it is not (Tanner, 1990, I, pp. 114–122). Among others it is not just a union by grace, operation, or by equality of honor, or of supreme authority. It is not even a union by reference or relationship, by affection, or by power or simply on account of a good- will on part of the Word of God who is well pleased by being with humans. Furthermore, it is not by a union of confusion, or by an accidental union, as it were, for example, by joining a fourth person to the Holy Trinity (no 5) or by adoption, like we are, or by the way a man and wife becoming one in the flesh (no 14), or just by being in the body as in a temple (no 14). No, it is by way of synthesis, i.e., preserving its original feature as a 'composite,' opposite to a single, to a monad.

It is a union according to the hypostasis. It is a union in one person, which means that in Jesus there is only one personal grammatical subject of all propositions related to both the divine and human nature. The properties of both natures can and must be predicated of the one person of Jesus Christ. The Word of God is the one who became flesh and dwelt among us (cf Jn 1, 4). In Jesus there is a real communication of properties as was already understood by Ephesus when it stated that Mary is the mother of God because being born of a woman can and must be predicated of the one person, that is Jesus Christ, the Word of God.

Jesus Christ, God and man as ultimate reality and meaning, implies that the new ultimate reality and meaning is one grammatical subject of all the properties which can be predicated of an ultimate reality and meaning conceived as a God, or as a man. Here one can sense the close unity of incarnation (into the human world) and of the resurrection (into eternity). By incarnation the divine ultimate reality and meaning accepts denominations of human ultimate reality and meaning and by resurrection the human ultimate reality and

29

meaning accepts denominations of the divine ultimate reality and meaning. The invisible becomes visible and the temporal eternal. The secular enters the divine and the divine assumes the secular – a philosophy which is divine (theological philosophy), and a theology which is human (philosophical theology) – yet without change and confusion, without division and separation.

6.2.5

Constantinople III 680-681: In Jesus Christ There Are Two Real Wills, Divine and Human (No Theandric Will)

The participants of Constantinople III were surprised that the previous 'five holy and Ecumenical' councils were not enough. They failed to realize that councils will be necessary so long as the Church lives in this world. On account of the unlimited question-raising function of the human mind any solution given will open new questions which for the Church in the final analysis continue to be Christological ones.

The Monothelites argued that if there is one subject in Christ there must be one energy, one will. The question was what a real subject really means. To reinforce the unity of Christ the previous councils removed the man in Christ as the final grammatical subject of all propositions and actions and replaced it by the Word as the final subject of all his statements and actions. The Monothelites used a similar sort of removal-replacement problem-solving paradigm to safeguard the perfect harmony and unity between the human and divine will of Christ: they removed human will in Christ and replaced it by the divine will.

When in response Constantinople III extended the Chalcedon principle to the will of Jesus Christ, sc. that in him the two natural operations and wills, the divine and human, are united not only indivisibly and inseparably but also without change and confusion (Tanner, 1990, I, p. 128), it reaffirmed the human reality of Christ as ultimate reality and meaning. For not just Christ's 'flesh,' but the natural will of his flesh also belongs to the Word of God. As his flesh so his natural human will was not absorbed by the divine, but rather validated in order to concur more fittingly for the salvation of the human race. In other words, not the unknowable will of an invisible God, but the human will and the intentionalities of the visible Christ as he appeared during his earthly life are the revelation of God's will and intention and remain the standard of any human action and intentionality. The Gospel narratives, therefore, remain the way, the truth and life for anyone to be saved for ever.

The next Christo-'logical' step will be Nicaea II.

31

6.2.6

Nicaea II 787: Jesus Christ is Real God, Yet Can be Represented in Icons, Since as a Real Man He Can be Subjected to the Standard of Human Arts and of Other Human Disciplines

Is it possible to represent ultimate reality and meaning? If, as in the Old Testament, the invisible God is still the ultimate reality and meaning the answer is no. And the iconoclasts with the emperor Leo III are right. But if Jesus Christ the real God and real man is ultimate reality and meaning, then the answer is yes and Pope Gregory III and Nicaea II are right. Though one can say with Theophanes that the second council of Nicaea did really not proclaim anything new, yet understood some further implication of the Nicaean Creed and let Christ enter deeper into the realms of human endeavors (Tanner, 1990, I, pp. 135–137). With the same logic Constantinople IV advanced in the direction taken by the Nicaean councils.

6.2.7

Constantinople IV 869-870: Jesus Christ is Invisible and Visible, Incomprehensible and Comprehensible, Not Confined (to a Limited Space, *Incircumscriptus*) and Confined (to a Limited Space, *Circumscriptus*), Therefore, Cannot Be and Can Be Inscribed in Other Human Conditions and Circumstances (*Inscriptibilis et Scriptibilis*)

It is rather unfortunate that because of the Photius controversy Constantinople IV could not enjoy the same acceptance as the previous councils of Constantinople. In proper perspective, Constantinople IV is the culmination of the eastern Christological councils which opened the door for the western Christological councils beginning with Lateran I and presently ended with Vatican II. It is Constantinople IV's profession that Christ is 'confined and not confined' to any space, to any system or mind-set that will lead us in our attempt of discovering Christological interpretations and see all the subsequent councils as the further ramifications of Nicaea I.

According to the 'Definition' taken from the Roman edition, the fourth council of Constantinople repeats and approves the second council of Nicaea 'when it professed the one and the same Christ as both invisible and visible, incomprehensible and comprehensible,' not confined to a limited space (*incircumscriptus*) and confined to a limited space (*circumscriptus*), incapable and capable of suffering, cannot be and can be (*inscriptibilis et scriptibilis*), inscribed in other human conditions and circumstances (Tanner, 1991, I, p. 162). Constantinople IV was just extending Nicaea II's principle from human arts to other human conditions, like space, mental system, etc., and thus reaffirming that Jesus Christ is real man and real God. This principle seems to be operating also in the discussion of the case of Photius, who could not see that Christ who is confined yet, at the same time, cannot be confined to Constantinople. Christ is confined and not confined to the East. In a right perspective Constantinople IV laid down the foundation of the principle of ecumenism formulated explicitly more than one thousand years later by Vatican II.

6.2.8

Lateran I (Investiture) 1123: Jesus Christ is Confined (Sceptre and Regalia) and Not Confined (Staff, Ring) to the Realm of the State

The principle operating in Nicaea II (on account of his humanity and divinity Christ is subjected to the standard of human arts and of other human disciplines) and Constantinople IV (confined and not confined to a limited space and to other human conditions and circumstances) helped to solve the problem of investiture. The bestowal of the regalia and sceptre, symbol of the power of the world over the subjects of the world, by the king, the head of the state, on a local leader of the Church, symbolizes that Christ, and consequently his Church too, being in the world, are subject to worldly power. Otherwise neither Christ nor the Church would be really human. Yet at the same time Christ, and consequently his Church, are not subject to the world. And this is expressed by the bestowal of the ring (seal of fidelity) and of the pastoral staff (sign of the pastoral activity) reserved to the pope, as the Vicar of Christ (Tanner, 1990, I, pp. 187, 190, 192).

It is noteworthy that Lateran I had been accepted as an ecumenical council, whereas others, from the point of doctrine, more important councils, like the Council of Carthage condemning Pelagius in 416, and the Council of Orange II proclaiming the primacy of grace in 529, were not. An ecumenical council means, therefore, more than just infallible teaching. Considered from the point of view of theological precision of concepts and of more adequate theological vocabulary the Council of Carthage in 416 and the Council of Orange in 529 were more elaborate than the Lateran Councils. Yet from the point of view of Nicaean hermeneutics, i.e., that Jesus Christ as ultimate reality and meaning is confined and not confined to certain territories, the Lateran Councils can be more 'eye-opening' for the Church in grasping Christ's presence in the world than the well-known teaching of the Scripture that apart from Christ it can do nothing (Jn 15, 5).

6.2.9

Lateran II (Simony) 1139: Jesus Christ is Confined (Sustenance for the Clergy) and Not Confined to the Realm of Money (Christ is Not For Sale)

One reason for calling the second Lateran Council was to end somehow the schism of Anacletus and confirm Innocent II as the true successor of Peter. The first two canons condemn making financial profit by using grace and spiritual power which Christ gave to his Church. But the council of Lateran II is neither the first nor the last to forbid simony. The council of Chalcedon forbade it already and the third Lateran Council in 1179 did the same. Yet there is some special reason for selecting simony as the key word for a Christological interpretation of the second Lateran Council.

Due to its rising wealth the Church became more worldly. The world became increasingly affluent and the Church with it by entering the road which led to the top of its this-worldly power with Innocent III. There was a new experience of wealth with a new task to learn how much Jesus Christ is confined and not confined to wealth and money.

Stressing the humanity of Christ Lateran II censured the 'Monophysite' spiritualist reform promoted by Arnold of Brescia. It condemned also the followers of Henry of Lausanne, a precursor of the Waldensians (Tanner, 1990, I, p. 196), another spiritualist movement. But at the same time it placed the condemnation of simony at the top of its canons. The Church needs the money, because it has to live in this world (to build Churches, and have more than the necessaries of life for imitating God's generosity in giving) yet no one should be able to buy Christ and his grace and thus 'deliver God to slavery.' Christ is confined to money and is not confined to money. But the further precision of the meaning of this principle will remain the task of an ongoing learning process about Christ's presence in the world.

6.2.10

Lateran III (Holy War) 1179: Jesus Christ is Confined (Cleaning up the Temple, 'I Have Come To Bring a Sword,' Cursing the Fig Tree) and not Confined to the Realm of Self-Defense by Physical Force (Turn the Other Cheek)

As earlier for both the ones affirming and the ones denying the divinity of Christ so too the Bible lended support for the partisans of holy war and the refusers of using any physical force. We should notice though that the Popes and the Councils justifying wars were citing more the Old Testament than the New. The declaration of the 'Holy War' can, indeed, be considered as a great novelty (Vernet, 1925, col. 2649) but the most tragic outcome of this interpretation of Christ's humanity was Innocent's bull *Ad extirpanda* in 1251, permitting the use of torture by the Inquisition.

The Church through its councils progressively discovers by trial and not without oversight the implication of its basic hermeneutical principle, Jesus Christ. It is not always clear that, while I may be free to turn my left cheek to any one who strikes me on the right cheek (Mt 5, 39), I am free also to let any one strike my neighbor. Liberation theology tried to justify revolution and use of force as defence of the poor against the aggression which deprives the legitimate right of the oppressed (Boff, 1985). And Vatican II affirmed that a 'person in extreme necessity has the right to take from the riches of others what is necessary for personal sustenances' (*Gaudium et Spes*, no. 69; Tanner, 1990, II, p. 1118).

The wars against heretics, at least in intention, were not wars of aggression for the propagation of faith, but a self-defense, or more precisely, the defense of Jesus of Nazareth's right against unjust aggressors (see council of Lyons II). Self-defense was the professed reason for the house arrest of the Jews during the paschal feast in order to prevent them from ridiculing the Christian ceremonies, and the Saracens together with the Jews from mixing by mistake with Christian women, or Christians from mixing by mistake with Jewish and Saracen women. The more so, since such a custom was practiced already in some provinces for Moses himself enjoined upon his people to be 'distinguished in public from other people by the character of their dress' (Lev. 19,19; Dt 22, 5; 22, 11; Lateran IV, chapter 68, Tanner, 1990, I, p. 266).

So was the fight against heretics considered as a war against unjust aggressors. This note is not meant to be a defence for all that Christians committed against their neighbors. It is just a further confirmation that at least in official writings of the Church Jesus Christ never ceased to be looked upon as a problem solving paradigm. Though the intentions of the various members of the councils were not always Christian, the decrees are the proofs that Christ was never left completely out of the picture. Perhaps this is why that no council has ever incorporated in its texts Innocent IV 's Bull of *Ad extirpanda*. One could venture to say that the mystery of Christ solves anomalies by intensifying them in order to manifest its own unsurpassable problem- solving power throughout history.

6.2.11

Lateran IV (Transubstantiation) 1215: Jesus Christ is Confined (Bread and Wine in the Eucharist) and Not Confined to the Realm of the Material World (Sacraments Signify)

The seventy chapters of Lateran IV are introduced by a profession of faith, aimed at the Cathari and Albigenses who akin to Manichaean doctrine were expecting liberation from the body through redemption. Since they challenged the Nicaean ultimate reality and meaning of Jesus as real man, the council was a welcome occasion to reinstate the mystery of Christ's confinement and not confinement to the material world and to its language: 'His body and blood are truly contained in the sacrament of the altar under the forms of bread and wine, the bread and wine having been changed in substance (*transubstantiatis*)' (Tanner, 1990, I, p. 230). Nicaea II recognized that Jesus Christ is real God, yet as a real man he can be subjected to the standard of human arts and other human disciplines. Now Lateran IV finds that language and grammar are not exceptions. Christ's reality can be expressed in non-biblical language which as a result receives new meanings. As earlier during the council of Nicaea when it was felt necessary to use a non-biblical word, sc., *homoousios* (of the same essence) in order to reconcile the faith in one God with the worship of Jesus Christ, now Lateran IV introduced the word 'transubstantiation' to defend the Church's worship of the Eucharist. Without transsubstantiation the worship of the Eucharist would be plain idolatry. And again the meaning of the term is not to be taken from philosophical or Latin dictionaries but from the context of the Lateran creed, which determines the meaning of the word transubstantiation. 'In order to achieve this mystery of unity' (Tanner, 1990, I, p. 230), that Jesus Christ, and no one else and nothing else, is both the priest and the sacrifice, the word 'transubstantiation' was needed. Otherwise the Church would not be able to offer Christ with Christ to God, but only bread and wine in themselves of no particular value.

6.2.12

Lyons I (Formal Deposition of Frederick II) 1245: Jesus Christ is Confined and Not Confined to the Power of the Church

Due to his personality, talent and willpower Innocent III was able to enforce his authority over kings and heads of states. His success prompted the impression that since Christ is the priest-king of the New Testament the Church is entitled to exercise supreme power over world. No king is king unless the Church says so. In the light of this view Innoncent IV induced the council to depose Frederick II. But Frederick II remained emperor until his death and the power of the world prevailed. The incarnation did not empty the world of its power and it seems that the great commandment of the risen Christ that 'All authority in heaven and on earth has been given to me, go, therefore, and make disciples of all nations' (Mt 28, 18–19) did not intend that the Church become the superpower of the world.

The correct meaning of Jesus Christ as the real God and real man is to be discovered by the Church again and again. In this learning process the trial and error method is not excluded. It is a method of finding the way to reach a desired end by true human beings. For power in the world the pope and the council could argue with Mt 16. 19 and with the idea of the Vicar of Christ. Yet the correct Christological meaning of those words and of the twenty-seven Constitutions of the council had to be learned by the coming generations.

The divine nature of Christ did not make human nature inert. In seeking to do his Father's will he was not necessarily exempt from a human way of acting as, for example, making choices by a system of trial and error. And the Church is not different. The infallibility of the Church really means that the Church infallibly finds the ways to carry out the mandate of Christ and reach the given result, i.e, the salvation of the world. The infallibility of the Church, therefore, means much more than the infallibility of defining dogmas. The latter is an essential element of a more universal infallibility operating constantly in the Church.

6.2.13

Lyons II (Crusades) 1274: Jesus Christ is Confined (*Funiculus Hereditatis*) and Not Confined to the Holy Land

The last decree, no. 71 of the fourth Lateran Council called the crusade *negotium Christi* 'Jesus Christ's business' (Tanner, 1990, I, p. 268) and the council of Lyons II declared the Holy Land the Lord's inheritance *funiculus hereditatis dominicae* (Tanner, 1990, I, p. 309). The expression *funiculus hereditatis* is found in Ps 104,11 'I give you the land of Canaan as your portion for inheritance' and in Ps. 77, 54 *in funiculo distributionis* 'making a heritage for each.' *Funis, funiculus,* means cord or string linking something e.g., a heritage, to someone. Thus the theological reasoning for the Crusade was that the Holy Land belongs to Christ. It is his possession, therefore, it was a great injustice committed against him when the land was lost to the Saracens. On the basis of his just ownership and justice the Church wanted to regain the Land for Christ.

The question was again, what does it mean that Christ is a real man who, on one hand, paid tax to the administrator of his native land, and on the other, he is God who created the world, therefore, the whole world is his own? Is the Holy Land the Lord's heritage more than any other part of the world? If it is, who is his 'just' administrator, the pope or the head of the people living there? Is the Lord confined to his native country more than to any other country? After his death is he not more present under the eucharistic species in any sanctuary of his Church than in the Holy Land? With Lateran IV and with Trent the Church believes that Jesus Christ is 'truly, really and substantially' (Tanner, 1990, II, p. 697) present in the sacrament of the Eucharist, therefore, one must say the obvious, i.e., that Jesus Christ is not confined to the Holy Land. After the institution of the Eucharist is the relevance of the Holy Land not greatly diminished? This is a point the theologians of the Crusades failed to appreciate. Only after the unsuccessful outcome of the Crusades did the Church learn more about what it means that Jesus Christ is real man like any other human being and real God as God, the creator of the world.

Somewhat more meaningful motivation for the Crusade was the second mentioned by the second Council of Lyons, i.e., the gratitude, the love and affection for Jesus Christ and for his homeland. For the great benefit he provided for the human race as a Redeemer, he deserved the great love of those who were willing to leave their home to defend his cause (cf. the full pardon for the sin of those who show such a great sign of love and gratitude, Tanner, 1990, I, p. 312). A love for Jesus Christ includes the love of the Holy Land. But for such a love does it really matter who is the worldly lord of that land? The question is more appropriate since after the resurrection the whole world is Christ's homeland and the love of the Holy Land is the love of the whole earth, the symbol of which is the Holy Land.

During the last session of the council the *Filioque*, the procession of the Holy Spirit not only from the Father but from the Son as well, was discussed and approved. The *Filioque* dispute between west and east is more than just a linguistic, philosophical and political issue. It is a question whether Jesus Christ is rightly accepted as ultimate reality and meaning. Whereas the *non-Filioque* theology suggests the Father as someone to be found beyond the Son, the *Filioque* conveys more than just the equality between the Son and the Father. It underlines the reality of Jesus Christ as the ultimate reality and meaning, sc., the one who is not to be reduced or related to anyone or to anything outside of himself. The *Filioque* theology contemplates Christ as real God ('He who has seen me has seen the Father,' Jn 14,9) whereas the *non-Filioque* theology visualizes him more as not the ultimate ('the Father is greater than I am,' Jn 14, 28).

6.2.14

Vienne (Prescriptions of the Studies of Languages) 1311–1312: Jesus Christ is Confined and Not Confined to One Language

In our 'Christ as ultimate reality and meaning' hermeneutical interpretation of the councils we take up certain issues in order to test our hypothesis. But the validity of the hypothesis does not depend on the validity of the selection. Any topic could be tested to check how URAM Christology is operating in the outcome of the disputes. As any paradigm, ultimate reality and meaning on the one hand, illuminates issues, inspires new insight yet at the same time, on the other, it is open-ended enough to leave other areas and all sorts of problems for qualified experts to work on and to resolve (Kuhn, 1970, p. 10).

The closer we come to Vatican II the more divergent the topics of the following councils become. The council of Vienne too had various agenda like the freedom of the Church during the popes' exiles in Avignon, the question of the Order of Templars suppressed by Philip the Fair, observance of poverty of the Franciscans and the teaching of John Peter Olivi denying that the human soul was directly and per se the 'form' of the body. By rejecting Peter Olivi's thesis the council did not solemnly define a philosophical doctrine, but expressed its belief that Christ was a real man and therefore his soul was not just dwelling in his body in a sort of Platonic subsistential sense but in a real Aristotelian substantial sense. In other words, it wanted to express the unity of a man or woman with his/her soul and body as well as the unity of soul and body to stress the redemption of the body and not only of the soul.

The reconquest of the Holy Land was still on the agenda, but a new form of missionary method was promoted mostly on the motion of Raymond Lull. Following Christ's example 'who wished that his apostles, going through the whole world to evangelize, should have a knowledge of every tongue' (Decree 24, Tanner, 1990, I, p. 379) the Council prescribed that an abundant number of Catholics be well versed in the languages of the infidels and be able to present the faith adequately to them. This is the most lasting heritage of the council of Vienne. But it took many years until Vatican II was able to realize the full meaning, the *sensus plenior* of the twenty fourth decree of the council of Vienne.

6.2.15

Constance (Ending the Great Schism of the Three Popes) 1414-1418: Jesus Christ is Confined and Not Confined to the Local Church, to the Universal Church and to the Head of the Universal Church

The council of Constance which was to solve the problem of a Church having three popes at the same time, shows the dynamics of the interplay between the local Church and the universal Church and respectively between their heads the individual bishops, members of the episcopal community and the pope. The local Church, as the Church of Christ the real God and real man, has an inner tendency to become the universal Church and the universal Church for the same reason tries to be concrete and incarnated in the here and now of each local Church. As the local bishop represents the unity of the universal Church appearing in the local Church, the episcopal college represents the universal Church as the totality of the local Churches and the pope, the unity of the universal Church appearing in the local Churches. (Rahner, 1965, pp. 20–30). On account of the presence of Christ in the Church each local Church has a tendency to become what the Roman Church is now, sc., the symbol of the unity of all the Churches and each bishop has the intentionality of becoming the pope. This is why each Church can consider itself a 'Roman Church' and each bishop a papal bishop.

This interplay came to the fore more visibly at the council of Constance when three local bishops, the three popes and the community of the local bishops experientially tested how much Jesus Christ is confined and not confined to each one of them respectively and how the tendency toward unity is operating in their mutual diversity. By virtue of the unity existing in the dualism of Christ's finite humanity and infinite divinity, the Church is endowed with a twofold tendency towards unity: the singular to universal and the universal to singular. And this twofold tendency is appropriately expressed by the papal primacy and episcopal community differentiation. 'It seems that a Church with episcopal and papal differentiation can be an adequate expression of the unity of a Church endowed not with a single but with a twofold tendency towards unity.' (Horvath, 1971, p. 46). Much later Vatican I and Vatican II expressed in words the differentiated unity which was operative at Constance. One more step in grasping the mystery of Christ as the ultimate reality and meaning of the Church.

6.2.16

Basel-Ferrara-Florence-Rome (Unions) 1431-1445: Jesus Christ is Confined and Not Confined to One Rite of the Geographic and Linguistic Districts of the World.

The central concern and ambition of the council of Florence was union with as many groups as possible. The success, real or apparent, was considered as a criterion of validity. Both the council and the pope were eager to bring about more and more unions. There were unions with the Greeks, Armenians, Copts, Syrians, Chaldeans, Maronites. In addition, the Latin, Armenian and Arabic languages were used for the first time. 'Do not be an accepter of persons or of blood ties or of homeland or nation. All people are children of God and have been equally entrusted to you' are the words the first cardinal is expected from now on to address the pontiff 'publicly in a loud voice' every year on the anniversary of his election or coronation (Form of Consent, Tanner, 1990, I, pp 497, 496). 'Nobody shall in the future dare to call ... any individual among them, heretic(s) ... '(*Bull of Union with the Chaldeans and the Maronites of Cyprus,* Tanner, 1990, I, p. 591).

Rite is more than a simple difference in language and geographical location. It is a liturgical, spiritual and theological patrimony of living out one particular church's life of faith (Zuzek, 1989, p. 293) in Jesus Christ as the ultimate reality and meaning. The recognition of Greek, Armenian, Copt, Syrian, Chaldean, Maronite etc. rites is the apprehension of a Christ not confined to one's own way of living out faith, to one's own rite. It is a discovering him as the ultimate reality and meaning of the Roman Catholic, of the Greek, Armenian, Copt, Syrian etc., rites breaking through and opening particular horizons set by each one's own culture.

But councils do not change the present at once. Rather they anticipate the future. The aim of Florence became the task of Vatican II and will be a criterion of success for the councils to come. Councils are infallible not independently of each other but in their collectivity based on Nicaea and continuously building on each other. And this is truly 'the Lord's doing' (*Bull of Union with the Armenians,* Tanner, 1990, I, p. 535).

6.2.17

Lateran V (Neoplatonism) 1512-1517: Jesus Christ is Confined and Not Confined to the Culture of an Age (Renaissance).

Emerging emancipation from the culture of the age, shared also by Luther, was the moving force behind the condemnation of Neoplatonic philosophy in 1513 by reaffirming that the soul is not one for all human beings, but one for each, and is immortal (Tanner, 1990, I, p. 605). Yet this is not a natural condition of the soul, as later Baius said, and was condemned in 1567 for it (DS 1978), but a gift of Christ's grace.

An initial, but not too effective detachment from the culture of the age can be detected also in the *Bull on Reform of the Curia* urging the cardinals 'not to attract blame by display or splendor or superfluous equipment or in any other way' by having, for example, a great number of 'personal attendants and horses' (Tanner, 1990, I, pp. 618–619). One can sense here the beginning of the end of the renaissance splendor, yet it is still a long way to Vatican II when the pope has left his tiara and sedan. Nevertheless it is noteworthy that Lateran V at the same time defended the *Montes pietatis*, a sort of charitable organization for lending money to the poor in case of necessity. This was the first step of entering the new culture of capitalism, which was coming to replace the feudalism of the renaissance.

Both the Neoplatonism and the renaissance had something in common with Christ. As distinct cultures they were means to control or cope with the contingencies of time and as such playing Christ's role. Yet both failed. They could not replace Christ, because Christ as the real God and the real man could not be identified with either one. Being an 'anomaly' for all, he prompts a shift of paradigms throughout history. Christ is confined and not confined to any culture of history.

6.2.18

Trent (Synthesis of the Augustinian {Lutheran} and Thomistic Theologies) 1545–1563: Jesus Christ is Confined and Not Confined to One Theological System (cf. Subsequent Elaboration of the Various Theological Notes)

The council of Trent was the first council which covered almost the entire span of theology. It was a council of the theologians and concerned with doctrines rather than with peoples, condemning statements rather than persons. Luther was on the mind of many of the participants yet his name was never mentioned in the decrees of the council. It is in this tradition that Vatican II did not mention names.

The two schools, the Augustinian-Franciscan-Jesuit, on the one side, and the Dominican on the other, were involved and tried to bring to the council the best of their traditions. The balance of the 'and' and 'and,' employed already by the fist council of Nicaea, became the paradigm of what is called the 'orthodox' Roman Catholic doctrine. Whereas the Arian 'only' ('*solus*' '*sola*' '*solum*') man and not God remained the heritage of the analytical philosophical mind in search for an exclusively univocal clarity of the 'yes' or 'no.'

The preparation preceding the justification and the true nature of justifications, the human and the divine, extolled more by one school than the other, found its way to the council and at the end came out as a new symbiosis reflecting once more the union of the truly man and truly God Jesus Christ. When the Augustinian, Franciscan, Jesuit, Thomist Fathers and theologians went to Trent, each of them had a personal 'updated' view of the Church and of its task in that age. But none of them came out the way they went in. During the council they discovered that their words, their language, carried a deeper sense and had a more comprehensive message that was not just Augustinian, Franciscan, Suarezian, or Thomist, but the voice of a much larger universal church extending the mystery of the incarnated Christ in time and space. They discovered that not everything is as clear and simple as they thought. There are shades of evidence and certitude, degrees of clarity which explain one's view and give leeway for others. And this was the importance of the theological notes. A rather rigorous and simplistic view of others' mind could open itself to ponder opposing views with freedom, tolerance and appreciation (cf. religious freedom acknowledged by Vatican II).

6.2.19

Vatican I (Faith is Supernatural as well as Reasonable; Infallibility of the Pope) 1869–1870: Jesus Christ is Confined (Infallibility of the Church) and Not Confined to the Community as a Totality of Individuals (Infallibility of the Pope as One Individual Member of the Community)

Vatican I had two main issues. One was the nature of faith and the other the infallibility of the pope. In the first it is easy to recognize the Nicaean ultimate reality and meaning. Faith is supernatural and reasonable since Christ is real God and real man. It is much less clear how the same principle of understanding operates in the dogma of the infallibility of the pope.

We should admit that Christ lives in the Church, his mystical body which receives certain characteristics of its head. And one of them is Christ's infallibility based on his being the perfect and definitive revelation of God. 'Nobody knows the Father, except the Son and all those to whom the Son chooses to reveal him' (Mt 11, 27). Christ has a comprehensive knowledge of any word, expression, action, being, etc. and their power to symbolize God. Being real God and real man he is able to know God and the created world. He knows humans and their world, precisely in their deepest mystery sc., being revelations of God.

And this infallible knowledge of the world and of his own being as revelation of God is shared by the Church. The Church's infallibility, therefore, is not a surface knowledge of the world accessible to us by talent and studious effort. Rather it is a knowledge of a deeper level, where the Church is able to recognize certain words, expressions, actions, as the adequate and unambiguous symbols, firstly of its own self, being a community of faith, charity and hope, and as such the sacrament of Christ, and secondly, of the generosity of the Father, the integrity of the Son and the authenticity of the Holy Spirit, the mystery of the Trinitarian God.

The awareness of this infallibility existed from the beginning. What Vatican I had expressed about Christ's mystery of incarnation was that Christ is not confined to the community of the Church as a totality of individuals. What he is to the totality he can also be to one individual member of that community who can share his infallibility, not independently of the community yet truly as an individual. If we abide in him, his words can abide in us (Jn 15, 7). The papal infallibility is the revelation that Jesus can live not only in the Church as a community, but in each member of it. The uniqueness of the pope is the symbol of the uniqueness of each of us. There is a little pope in each of us. Paul's saying that he lives but it is not he but it is the Christ who lives in him (see Gal, 2, 20) can be applied to each of us. If we as individuals abide in him, he abides not only in the community, but in each individual, though not independently of the community (cf. Jn 15, 1–7).

Vatican I has laid down the foundation for coming councils concerned with the mystery of how Christ dwells in each of us: how is Christ confined and not confined to our community, and how is he confined and not confined to the 'spirit' of each us, that we can have a direct relation with him not through, but in the community. Christian life is a community life, yet it is always based on the inalienability of a person which no community can take away or absorb. A Christian always must remain free to be confined and not to be confined to the world – a freedom which the conciliar documents support.

6.2.20

Vatican II 1962-1965: Jesus Christ is Confined and Not confined to the Visible Institutional Church (the World as Vehicle of the Grace of the Church: Spatial Language); He is Confined and Not Confined to the Past (He has the Future as well: Temporal Language)

Vatican II was an experience for the Church recognizing that the world, though not independently of the Church, can be truly a vehicle of the grace which the Church has but not on its own. The Church's grace is not the Church's grace but Christ's grace. As Christ's teaching was his own, yet not his, but his who sent him (cf Jn 7, 16), so the Church now knows that the grace which it has is not its grace but his who sent it. This is why the Council could say that some, 'and most, of the significant elements and endowments which together go to build up and give life to the Church itself, can exist outside the visible boundaries of the catholic church' (*Decree on Ecumenism*, no. 3; Tanner, II, p. 910.). This lead us to a more comprehensive understanding of the Church. It is not only the Church of a few, but the Church of all since in various ways, all people are related to the Church, the people of God (*Dogmatic Constitution on the Church*, nos, 6, 13–17; Tanner, II, pp. 861, 859– 862). Therefore, non-Christian religions too belong to the Church and can become the vehicle of Christ's grace.

Christ was, is and will be present in the Church, yet his presence is not confined to its boundaries, since he is the Creator, the Lord and Saviour of all peoples. The Christ of Vatican II is the risen Christ who progressively without any delay until the last day extends his Kingdom in time and space by leading all peoples born in time to eternity. He is the eschatological Lord of the universal eschatological Church which being in time is already one with the Church in eternity. The tone of Vatican II, therefore, is not the tone of worries and complaints about the evil in the world. It is a joyful vibration of the resurrection. Instead of looking back and around, it looks ahead. It has a vision of the future which is a reality already. It is the vision of Mary the mother of Jesus Christ, in her bodily and spiritual glory, as a sure sign and pledge of the Church's optimism. And this optimism is not limited to chapter eight of the *Dogmatic Constitution on the Church*. It permeates all sixteen documents. It is a vision of Christ who is confined and not confined to space or time. He is that real man and real God whom the Council of Nicaea I confessed as the ultimate reality and meaning of all.

7.
Conclusion

The text of the twenty-one Ecumenical Councils makes sense in secular contexts without any religious or Christological interpretation. Words, sentences, paragraphs, chapters, as well as the complete text of one single or all the twenty-one councils together, can be interpreted as any literary, historical, psychological, sociological work of a group of people. And these interpretations are true in the sense of the discipline involved. They are conditioned by the idea of ultimate reality and meaning of the interpreting author and may be assumed by the specific discipline in question. They are, therefore, constantly developing since the conciliar texts, as any other texts, have the power of making different impacts on the mind of their readers prompting favorable and unfavorable reactions alike.

And all this is legitimate. The texts are made up by humans who addressed them to other human beings, Jesus Christ not excluded. Otherwise, the authors would have not recognized with the council of Nicaea the true man Jesus Christ as the ultimate reality and meaning. And this justifies the conciliar theologian's dialogue with any scientist or any human being, religious or not religious about the meaning of the conciliar texts.

By similar reasoning one has to admit that, in addition to the secular context, the same words, sentences, paragraphs, chapters as well as the complete text of one single or of all twenty-one councils together, make sense in a religious context too. There is an authentic religious concern which can be found meaningful in the context of almost any religion. And this justifies conciliar theologian's dialogue with any religion or religious men and women eager to learn more about their own religion, the religion of others, and even more, about themselves and others.

But neither the secular nor the religious interpretation can exhaust the full meaning of the conciliar texts. The Christological interpretation opens a further dimension of meaning proper only to the conciliar texts. We find that this interpretation is simple, plausible, coherent, consistent and explains more obscurities in the texts. It explains not only the doctrinal and organizational statements, but the numerous canons, instructions, exhortations, disciplinary

Conclusion

measures and threats aiming at the reform of the church not-withstanding all the previous failures. In spite of the ever-lasting problems of celibacy, the seemingly inefficient reprobations of immorality, the pride, the quarrels, and the ever-returning sins and irregularities, the never-ceasing effort and hope for renewal would not make sense unless Christ remained from the first council to the last one a model and guiding principle for solving problems. The Christological interpretation of the counciliar documents does not regard only the ad-hoc of the present or the past but opens the future. It seems, indeed, to have most of the characteristics of the best explanation (cf. Banner, 1990, pp. 119–153).

Jesus Christ as ultimate reality and meaning is one of the various possible Christological interpretations of the council documents. It is presented here to interested readers to test its power on any texts of the twenty-one Ecumenical Councils. The text selected should be placed successively in a secular, religious and Christological context and evaluated not just by the problem-solving (Kuhn, 1970. p. 10) but also by the meaning-opening power of the hermeneutical principle of Jesus Christ, the real man and real God, as ultimate reality and meaning.

References

1. Texts

Acta Synodalia Sacrosancti Concilii Documenti Vaticani II. 1970–1980. Vatican City.

Alberigo, J., J.A. Dosseti, P-P. Joannou, C. Leonardi, P. Prodi and H. Jedin. 1983. *Conciliorum Oecumenicorum Decreta.* Bologna: Instituto per le Science Religiose.

Ayer, J.C. 1941. *A Source Book for Ancient Church History.* New York: Charles Scribner.

Denzinger, H., A. Schönmetzer. 1963. *Enchiridion Symbolorum. Definitiones et Declarationes de Rebus Fidei et Morum.* New York: Herder.

Mansi, J.D. 1759–1927. *Sacrorum Conciliorum Nova et Amplissima Collectio.* Paris: H. Welter.

Neuner, J., J. Dupuis. 1975. *The Christian Faith in the Doctrinal Documents of the Catholic Church.* Westminster: Christian Classics Inc.

Schwartz, E. 1922–1940. *Acta Conciliorum Oecumenicorum.* Berlin: W. de Gruyter.

Tanner, N.P. 1990. *Decrees of the Ecumenical Councils.* Washington, D.C.: Georgetown University Press.

2. General History

Bettenson, H. 1967. *Documents of the Christian Church.* Oxford: Oxford University Press.

Davis, L.D. *The First Seven Councils (325–787). Their History and Theology.* 1987. Wilmington: Glazier.

Dvornik, F. 1961. *The Ecumenical Councils.* New York: Hawthorn Books.

Hefele, P., H. Leclerq. 1907-1938. *Histoire des Conciles d'après les Documents Originaux.* Paris: Letouzey et Ané.

Hughes, P. 1961. *The Church in Crisis: A History of the General Councils.* Garden City, NY.: Doubleday.

Jedin, H. 1960. *Ecumenical Councils of the Catholic Church* New York: Herder and Herder.

Jedin, H., J. Dolan. 1980. *History of the Church.* London: Burns and Oates.

Kelly, J. N.D. 1958. *Early Christian Doctrines.* London: Adam and Charles Black.

References

Schaff, P. 1974. *A Select Library of the Nicene and Post-Nicene Fathers of the Christian Church.* 14 vols. Grand Rapids, MI: Eerdmans.

Pelikan, J. 1970. *The Church Tradition I. Emergence of the Catholic Tradition (100–600).* Chicago: University of Chicago Press, pp. 172-278.

Raab, C. 1959. *The Twenty Ecumenical Councils of the Catholic Church.* Westminster: The Newman Press.

Stevenson, J. 1966. *Creeds, Councils and Controversies.* London: *S.P.C.U.*

Swetman, J. 1978. 'The Geography of Dogma I, II, III, IV, V, VI' *America.* pp. 101, 123, 146, 169, 190, 212.

3. Twenty-One Ecumenical Councils

3.1 Nicaea I – 325

Bright, W. 1882. *Notes on the Canons of the First Four General Councils.* Oxford: Clarendon Press, pp. 1–78.

Burn, A.E. 1925. *The Council of Nicaea.* London: S.P.C.K.

Grillmeier, A. 1989. *Jesus Christus in Glauben der Kirche.* Freiburg: Herder, Band 2/2, pp. 451–620.

Honigmann, E. 1936. 'Recherches sur les listes des pères de Nicée et de Constantinople.' *Byzantion* 11:429–449.

Newman, J.H. 1833. *The Arians of the Fourth Century.*

Ortiz de Urbina, I. 1963. *Nicée et Constantinople.* Histoire des Conciles Oecuméniques. Paris: Editions de l'Orante, pp. 15–36.

Schröder, H.J. 1937. *Disciplinary Decrees of the General Councils.* St. Louis, MO: Herder.

3.2 Constantinople I – 381

Bringt, W. 1882. *Notes on the Canons of the First Four General Councils.* Oxford:Clarendon, pp. 79–108.

Hanson, R.P.C. 1983. 'The Holy Spirit in Creeds and Confessions of Faith in the Early Church' *Credo in Spiritum Sanctum.* Vatican City: Libreria Editrice Vaticana, pp. 291–302

Kannengisser, C. 1981. 'Athanasius of Alexandria and the Holy Spirit Between Nicaea I and Constantinople I.' *Irish Theological Quarterly.* 48:166–180.

King, N.Q. 1957. 'The 150 Holy Fathers of the Council of Constantinople 381 A.D. Somes Notes on the Bishops-lists' *Studia Patristica* 1:635–641.

Ortiz de Urbina, I, 1963. *Nicée et Constantinople.* Paris: Editions de l'Orante, pp. 139–242.

Ritter, A.M. 1965. *Das Konzil von Konstantinopel und sein Symbol.* Göttigen: Vandenhock and Ruprecht

Zizioulas, J.D. 1983. 'The Teaching of the 2nd Ecumenical Council on the Holy Spirit in Historical and Ecumenical Perspective.' *Credo in Spiritum Sanctum.* Vatican City: Libreria Editrice Vaticana, pp. 29–54.

3.3 Ephesus – 431

Aprem, M. 1978. *Council of Ephesus of 431*. Trichur, India: Mar Narsai Press.
Camelot, P. 1962. *Ephese et Chalcédone*. Histoire des Conciles Oecuméniques. Paris: Editions de l' Orante.
McEnerey, J.I. 1987. *St. Cyril of Alexandria. Letters 1–50*. Washington: Catholic University of America Press.
Scipioni, L.I. 1974. *Nestorio e il concilio de Epheso*. Milan: Vita e Pensiero.

3.4 Chalcedon – 451

Grillmeier, A. 1962. *Das Konzil von Chalkedon*. Würzburg: Echter Verlag.
Sellers, R.V. 1953. *The Council of Chalcedon. A Historical and Doctrinal Survey*. London: SPCK.
Young, F. 1983. *From Nicaea to Chalcedon*. Philadelphia: Fortress Press.

3.5 Constantinople II – 553

Moeller, C. 1951. 'Le cinquième concile et le magistère ordinaire du 6ème siècle.' *Revue des sciences philosophiques et théologiques*. 35:413–423.
Murphy, F.X. 1974. *Constantinople II et Constantinople III*. Histoire des Conciles Oecuméniques. Paris: Editions de l'Orante.

3.6 Constantinople III – 680

Murphy, see above
Percival, H.R. Ed. 1974. "The Third Council of Constantinople." *The Seven Ecumenical Councils of the Undivided Church*, Gran Rapids, MI: U.M.B. Eerdmens, Nicene and Post Nicone Fathers, vol 14, pp. 325–352.

3.7 Nicaea II – 787

Alivastos, H.S. 1960. 'Les conciles Oecuméniques Ve, VIe, VIIe et VIIIe' *Le Concile et les Conciles*. Paris: Editions du Cerf, pp. 111–123
Bayes, N.H. 1951. 'The Icons before Iconoclasm.' *Harvard Theological Review*. 44:93–106.
Dumège, J. 1976. *Nicée II*. Histoire des Conciles Oecuméniques. Paris: Editions de l'Orante.
Jedin, H.1960. 'Iconoclasm and the Veneration of Images.' *Ecumenical Councils of the Catholic Church*. New York: Herder and Herder, pp. 50–55
Martin, E.J. 1978. *A History of the Iconoclastic Controversy*. New York: Macmillan.
Ouspensky, L. 1976. *Theology of Icon*. Crestwood, NY: St. Vladimir's Seminary Press.
Schönborn, C. von. 1976. *L'Icone du Christ: Fondements théologiques élaborés entre Ier et le IIe Concile de Nicée (325–387)*. Fribourg: Editions universitaires.

References

Sendler, E. 1981. *L'icone. Image de l' Invisible: Éléments de théologie, esthétique et techniques.* Paris: Desclée.

3.8 Constantinople IV – 869–870

Hussey, J. 1986. *The Orthodox Church in the Byzantine Empire.* Oxford: Oxford University Press.

Stiernon, D. 1967. *Constantinople IV.* Histoire des Conciles Oecuméniques. Paris: Editions de l' Orante.

3.9 Lateran I – 1123

Foreville, R. 1965. *Latran I, II, III, et Latran IV.* Histoire des Conciles Oecuméniques. Paris: Editions de l'Orante.

Mollat, M., P. Tombeur. 1974. *Les conciles Latran I à Latran IV.: Concordance, index, listes de fréquences, tables comparatives.* Conciles Oecuméniques Médiévaux 1. Leuven: Université Catholique de Louvain.

Morrison, K.F. 1978. *The Investiture Controversy. Issues, Ideals, and Results.* Huntington, NY: R.E. Krieger Pub. Co.

3.10 Lateran II – 1139

Poole, R.L. 1923. 'The English Bishops at the Lateran Council of 1139.' *English Historical Review* 3:61–63.

Cheney, C.R. 'The Numbering of the Lateran Councils of 1179 and 1212.' *Medieval Texts and Studies.* Oxford Clarendon Press, pp. 203–209.

3.11 Lateran III – 1179

Kuttner, S. 1957. 'Brief Note Concerning the Canons of the Third Lateran Council.' *Traditio.* 13:505–506.

Longère, J. 1982. *Le troisième concile du Latran (1179). Sa place dans l'histoire.* Paris: Etudes Augustiniennes.

Vernet, F. 1925. 'Latran III.' *Dictionnaire de théologie catholique,* vol. 8, 2, Paris: Letouzey et Ané, col. 2649

3.12 Lateran IV – 1215

Kuttner, S., A. Garcia y Garcia. 1964. 'A New Eyewitness Account of the Fourth Lateran Council.' *Traditio* 20:115–178.

Luchaire, A. 1980. 'Innocent III et le quatrième concile du Latran.' *Revue historique* 97:166–172.

3.13 Lyons I – 1245

Lunt, W. 1918. 'The Sources for the first Council of Lyons. 1245.' *English Historical Review*. 33:72–78.

Mollat M., P. Tombeur. 1974. *Les conciles Lyon I et Lyon II: Concordance, index, listes de fréquences, tables comparatives*. Conciles Oecuméniques. Louvain: Université Catholique de Louvain.

Wolter, H., H. Holstein. 1966. *Lyon I et Lyon II*. Histoire des Conciles Oecuméniques. Paris: Editions de l' Orante.

3.14 Lyons II – 1274

Emery, R.W. 1966. 'The Second Council of Lyons and the Mendicant Orders.' *Catholic Historical Review*. 39:257–272.

Geanakoplos, D.J. 1959. *Emperor Michael Paleologus and the West 1258–1282*. Cambridge, Mass: Harvard University Press.

3.15 Vienne – 1311–1312

Barber, M. 1978. *The Trial of the Temples*. Cambridge, Mass: Harvard University.

Leclerq, J. 1964. *Vienne*. 1964. Histoire des Conciles Oecuméniques. Paris: Editions de l'Orante.

3.16 Constance – 1414–1418

Crowder, C.M.D. 1977. *Unity, Heresy and Reform. 1378–1460*. London: Edward Arnold.

Gill, J. 1965. *Constance et Bale-Florence*, Histoire des Conciles Oecuméniques. Paris: Editions de l' Orante.

Jacob, E.F. 1943. *Essays on the Conciliar Epoch*. Manchester: Publications of the University, Historical Series 80.

Loomis, L.R. 1961. *The Council of Constance*. New York: Columbia University Press.

Spinka, M. 1965. *John Hus at the Council of Constance*. New York: Columbia University Press.

3.17 Florence – 1431–1445

Concilium Florentinum. Acta Graeca. 1953 Edited by J.Gill, *Acta Latina* 1959. Edited by G. Hoffmann. Rome: Pontificium Orientalium Studiorum.

Gill, J. *The Council of Florence*. 1959. Cambridge: Harvard University Press.

— 1964. *Personalities of the Council of Florence*. London: Oxford University Press.

3.18 Lateran V – 1512–1517

Bilaniuk, P. 1973. *The Fifth Lateran Council and the Eastern Churches*. Toronto: The Central Committee for the Defense of Rite.

Minnich, N.1982. 'Paride de Gravi's Diary of the Fifth Lateran Council.' *Annuarium Historiae Conciliorum*. 14:370–460.

References

Schoeck, R. 1981. 'The Fifth Lateran Council: Its Partial Successes and its Larger Failures.' *Reform and Authority in the Medieval and Reformation Church*. Edited by G. Little. Washington, D.C.: Catholic University Press, pp. 99–116.

3.19 Trent – 1545–1563

Concilium Tridentinum: Diariorum, Actorum, Epistolarum, Tractatuum nova collectio. 1901–1938. Freiburg: Görresgesellschaft.

Jedin, H. 1951. *A History of the Council of Trent*. St. Louis: Herder.

— 1957. *A History of the Council of Trent*. St. Louis: Herder.

— 1967. *Crisis and Closure of the Council of Trent: A Retrospective View from the Second Vatican Council*. London: Sheed and Ward.

Kremnitz, F.M.(1522–1586). 1971. *Examination of the Council of Trent*. St. Louis, MO: Concordia.

Leclerq, J, et al. 1981. *Trente*. Histoire des Conciles Oecuméniques. Paris: Editions de l' Orante.

Schroeder, H. J. 1967. *Canons and Decrees of the Council of Trent*. New York: Herder and Herder.

— 1937. *Disciplinary Decrees of the General Councils*. St. Louis, MO: Herder.

3.20 Vatican I – 1869–1870

Aubert, R. 1967. *Vatican I*. Histoire des Conciles Oecuméniques. Paris: Editions de l' Orante.

Hasler, A.B. 1981. *How the Pope Became Infallible*. New York: Doubleday.

Pottmeyer, H.J. 1968. *Der Glaube vor dem Anspruch der Wissenschaft*. Der Konstitution 'Dei Filius' des I Vatikanisches Konzils. Freiburg: Herder.

3.21 Vatican II – 1962–1965

Vorgrimler, H. Editor. 1967. *Commentary with the Documents of Vatican II*. New York: Herder and Herder.

4. Hermeneutics

Banner, M.C. 1990. *The Justification of Science and the Rationability of Religious Belief*. Oxford: Clarendon Press.

Boff, L. 1985. *Church: Charism and Power*. New York: Crossroad.

Breisach, E. 1983. *Historiography*. Chicago: University of Chicago Press.

Congar, Y. et al. 1960. *Le Concile et les Conciles*. Paris: les Éditions dulecf.

Grillmeier, A. 1975. *Christ in Christian Tradition*. Atlanta: J. Knox Press.

Horvath, T. 1971. 'The Sacrament of Ordination as Revelation of God.' *The Heythrop Journal*. 12:44–52.

— 1975. *Faith Under Scrutiny*. Notre Dame: Fides.

— 1977a. 'A Structural Understanding of the Magisterium of the Church.' *Science et Esprit*. 29:283–311.

— 1977b. 'Study of Man's Horizon-Creation: A Perspective for Cultural Anthropology.' *The Concept and Dynamics of Culture*. Edited by B. Bernardi. The Hague: Mouton Publishers, pp. 315–329.

— 1980. 'Structure of Scientific Discovery and Man's Ultimate Reality and Meaning.' *Ultimate Reality and Meaning* 3: 144–163.

Kuhn, T.S. 1970. *The Structure of Scientific Revolutions*. Chicago: University of Chicago Press.

Lonergan, B.F.J. 1976. *The Way to Nicea: the Dialectical Development of Trinitarian Theology*. London: Darton, Longman, Todd.

Meyendorff. J. 1973. 'What is an Ecumenical Council?' *St. Vladimir's Theological Quarterly*. 17: 259–273.

Rahner, K. 1965. 'The Episcopate and the Primacy' K. Rahner and J. Ratzinger. *The Episcopate and Primacy*. 1965. London, pp. 20–30.

— 1966. 'What is a Dogmatic Statement?' *Theological Investigations* 5, pp. 42–66.

— 1976. 'Basic Observations on the Subject of Changeable and Unchangeable Factors in the Church.' *Theological Investigations* 14, pp. 3–23.

— 1976. '*On the Concept of Infallibility in Catholic* Theology.' *Theological Investigations* 14, pp. 66–84.

— 1976. 'The Faith of the Christian and the Doctrine of the Church.' *Theological Investigations* 14, pp. 24–46.

— 1976. 'Does the Church Alter Any Ultimate Certainties?' *Theological Investigations* 14, pp.47–65.

Sieben, H.J. 1979. *Die Konzilidee der Alten Kirche*. Paderborn: F. Schöningh.

Story, C.K. 1981. 'Ultimate Reality and 'The Gospel of Truth."' *Ultimate Reality and Meaning* 4:279–296.

Strack, C.H.L., P. Billerbeck. 1922. *Kommentar zum neuen Testament aus Talmud und Midrash*. Münich: Oskar Beck, 1, 36–43).

Zuzek, I. 1989. 'The *Ecclesiae Sui Iuris* in the Revision of Canon Law.' *Vatican II. Assessment and Perspectives*. Edited by R. Latourelle. Mahwah, NJ.: Paulist Press, vol. 3, pp. 288–304.

Index